TALES OF INVENTION

THE TELEPHONE

Richard and Louise Spilsbury

Heinemann Library

Chicago, Illinois

© 2011 Heinemann Library
an imprint of Capstone Global Library, LLC
Chicago, Illinois

Edited by Louise Galpine and Laura Knowles
Designed by Philippa Jenkins
Original illustrations © Capstone Global Library Ltd 2011
Illustrated by KJA-artists.com
Picture research by Mica Brancic

Originated by Capstone Global Library Ltd
Printed and bound in China by CTPS

15 14 13 12 11
10 9 8 7 6 5 4 3 2 1

Library of Congress Cataloging-in-Publication Data
Spilsbury, Richard, 1963-
 The telephone / Richard and Louise Spilsbury.
  p. cm. -- (Tales of invention)
 Includes bibliographical references and index.
 ISBN 978-1-4329-3826-0 (hc) -- ISBN 978-1-4329-3833-8 (pb) 1. Telephone--History--Juvenile literature. 2. Cellular telephones--Juvenile literature. I. Spilsbury, Louise. II. Title.
 TK6165.S67 2011
 621.385--dc22
                                     2009049027

Acknowledgments
The author and publisher are grateful to the following for permission to reproduce copyright material: Alamy pp. **16** (© The Art Gallery Collection/Visual Arts Library [London]), **26** (© Stefan Sollfors); Getty Images pp. **7** (Hulton Archive), **8** (Dennie Cody), **9** (Science & Society Picture Library), **14** (Hulton Archive/Stock montage), **17** (Time Life Pictures/Mansell), **18** (Hulton Archive/Russell Knight), **20** (Hulton Archive/Galerie Bilderwelt) **21** (Fox Photos/Stacey), **25** (Photographer's Choice/Bo Tornvig); iStockphoto pp. **23** (© Aleksandar Jocic), **19 bottom left** (© charles taylor); Nokia p. **27**; Photolibrary pp. **4** (Imagestate/The Print Collector), **5** (North Wind Picture Archives), **10** (Imagestate/The Print Collector), **24** (Index Stock Imagery/David Bases); Science & Society Picture Library p. **12** (Science Museum); Shutterstock pp. **19 bottom right** (Christopher Dodge), **19 top** (3355m).

Cover photographs of an iPhone reproduced with permission of Getty Images/AFP/Frederic J. Brown and a group of businessmen watching inventor Alexander Graham Bell as he opens the New York–Chicago telephone line in 1892 reproduced with permission of Corbis/© Bettmann.

We would like to thank Ian Graham for his invaluable help in the preparation of this book.

CONTENTS

Look for these boxes

Biographies

These boxes tell you about the life of inventors, the dates when they lived, and their important discoveries.

Setbacks

Here we tell you about the experiments that didn't work, the failures, and the accidents.

EUREKA!

These boxes tell you about important events and discoveries, and what inspired them.

Any words appearing in the text in bold, **like this**, are explained in the glossary.

TIMELINE

2010—The timeline shows you when important discoveries and inventions were made.

BEFORE TELEPHONES

The invention of the telephone changed the world. Today, most people have a telephone at home and also probably have a cell phone to carry with them at all times. We use telephones to speak to friends and family across the road or across the world. Telephones help businesses do deals with each other over long distances. Telephones also save people's lives. Think about what it was like before you could simply call the police, an ambulance, or the fire department when you needed them! Can you imagine what life was like before the telephone was invented?

Long before telephones, most people worked close to where they lived and did not travel very often. They visited each other's houses or met in restaurants, markets, and other public places to pass on news. People also sent letters by horse, wagon, or ship.

Ships have to communicate with each other quickly. At one time the only way to do this was by using signal flags.

1746—Jean Nollet proves that electrical signals move fast

1740   1750   1760

During the 1800s, trains and **steamships** were developed and large factories were built. People traveled more and did business over a greater area. This meant they wanted ways of **communicating** more quickly over long distances. Many inventors started to work on machines that could carry messages or sounds. Several great inventors made important discoveries that eventually led to the invention of the telephone.

It took the speedy horses and riders of the Pony Express 10 days to carry letters nearly 3,000 kilometers (2,000 miles) across the United States.

5

ELECTRIC MESSAGES

In 1837 an American named Samuel Morse invented the first successful **telegraph**. Telegraph machines send messages as electric signals. **Electricity** is a type of energy that makes machines work. It flows from a power source, such as a **battery**, around a wire **circuit**. Morse also developed a code to use on his telegraph, so the messages could be understood.

To send a telegraph, you press a switch that completes a circuit. Electricity flows through wire to a machine where it makes a sounder click. When you release the switch, the gap in the circuit stops the **current** from flowing.

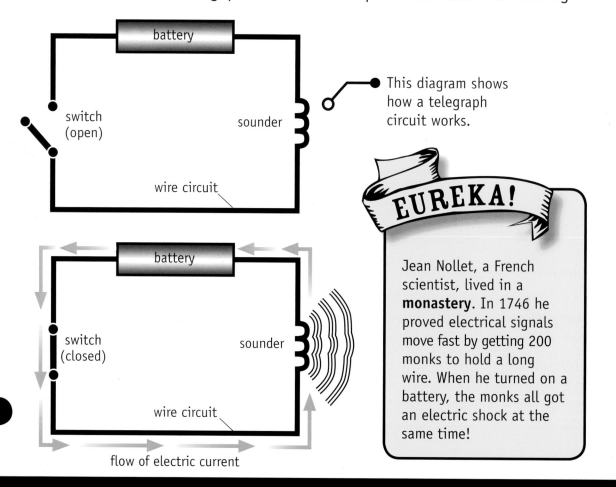

battery

switch
(open)

sounder

This diagram shows
how a telegraph
circuit works.

wire circuit

battery

switch
(closed)

sounder

wire circuit

flow of electric current

EUREKA!

Jean Nollet, a French scientist, lived in a **monastery**. In 1746 he proved electrical signals move fast by getting 200 monks to hold a long wire. When he turned on a battery, the monks all got an electric shock at the same time!

Morse Code

In Morse Code, a different combination of dots and dashes (long or short spaces between clicks) stands for each letter of the alphabet. A telegraph operator tapped out messages letter by letter. An operator at the other end listened to the clicks and turned the message back into words.

In 1843 the U.S. government paid Morse for a telegraph service between Baltimore and Washington, D.C. By the 1850s, many places were linked by telegraph, and the first undersea cables were laid to connect different countries.

Samuel Morse
(1791–1872)

Samuel Morse was a painter who became fascinated by electrical experiments after someone showed him some electric devices. He became rich and famous from his telegraph, and Morse Code was still used to call for help at sea until 1999.

Sending speech

After the **telegraph** was invented, the next step was to try to send spoken words along wires. Before inventors could do this, they had to understand how sound works.

Sounds happen when something **vibrates**. Vibrations are movements back and forth, or up and down. When you hit a drum, the drum skin vibrates. This makes the air around the drum skin vibrate, too. These air movements are called **sound waves**. Sound waves spread out like ripples on a pond. Our ears turn them into signals that the brain recognizes as the sound of the drum.

When you talk into a tin-can phone, string carries the vibrations to the other can. This vibrates, too, and reproduces sounds.

In 1856 Italian-American inventor Antonio Meucci set up a system of wires between his workshop and his sick wife's bedroom so they could speak. But Meucci was too poor to buy a **patent** for his telephone. A patent is issued to someone who invents something new so that other people do not copy it without permission.

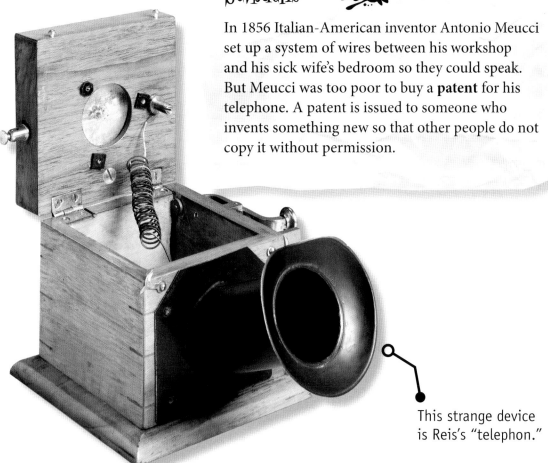

This strange device is Reis's "telephon."

First attempts

In 1854 a French scientist named Charles Bourseul wrote about using a vibrating metal disc to send speech, but he never built a machine to do it. In 1861 Johann Philipp Reis, a German scientist, tried to make a machine that used a metal disc to change sound vibrations into **electricity**. He called it a "telephon," from the Greek words *tele* meaning "distance" and *phone* meaning "voice," or "sound." It sent a few notes of music rather badly, but it could not carry speech.

9

1821—Michael Faraday invents the first electric motor

1827—William Sturgeon invents the **electromagnet**

1830

THE FIRST TELEPHONES

In 1876 Alexander Graham Bell became the first person to build a successful telephone and get a **patent** for it. Bell and a mechanic named Thomas Watson were working on ways to make **currents** copy **sound waves**. A current is the flow of **electricity** through a wire. Bell's first telephone used **acid** to do this. The next step would be to make a telephone without liquid, so that Bell could sell it to people.

Here, Bell and Watson are demonstrating how to use an early form of the telephone.

EUREKA!

Bell's first words over his telephone in 1876 were "Mr. Watson, come here, I want you." The story goes that Bell said this because he had spilled some acid on his leg! Watson had been in the other room with the telephone **receiver**. He said, "I heard every word."

10

1831—Michael Faraday shows that vibrations on metal objects can be turned into electrical signals

1837—Samuel Morse invents the first successful **telegraph** and the Morse Code

1840—The first postage stamp goes on sale

1830

1840

How it worked

Bell's first telephone had a funnel. This concentrated sounds onto a circle of sheepskin stretched over a frame, similar to a drum skin. A needle was attached to the sheepskin at one end and dipped in acid at the other. When Bell spoke into the funnel, sound waves made the sheepskin **vibrate**. This moved the needle in the acid. The tiny vibrations in the liquid changed the current in an electric wire. At the other end of the electric wire, there was an identical box that did everything in reverse and changed the vibrations back into words!

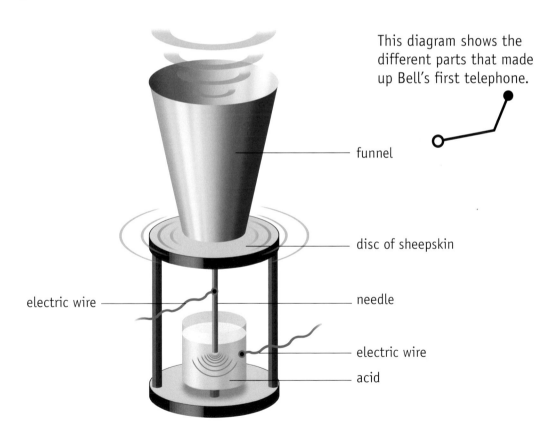

This diagram shows the different parts that made up Bell's first telephone.

funnel

disc of sheepskin

electric wire

needle

electric wire

acid

11

The next steps

Bell's liquid telephone was not practical and it did not transmit speech clearly, so he set about making a new telephone. This one used an **electromagnet** instead of liquid to change **sound waves** into electric **currents**. An electromagnet is a piece of metal that becomes magnetic when **electricity** flows through it. Magnetism is a force that pulls or pushes on certain metals.

Bell's telephone handset looked a bit like a stamp used to mark patterns on butter, so it became known as the butterstamp.

EUREKA!

In the 1820s, British electrical engineer William Sturgeon discovered that coiling a wire around a bar of iron and passing an electric current through the wire created an electromagnet. Today, electromagnets are used in many things, including televisions and electric motors.

Setbacks

To use the "butterstamp" telephone you had to talk into the handset and then move it to your ear to hear the reply. This confused a lot of people!

12

A working model

Inside each of Bell's wooden telephones was an electromagnet and a thin iron disc. When someone spoke into one of the handsets, sound waves made the disc **vibrate**. As the disc vibrated, it kept changing the strength of the electromagnet. This made a continuously changing electric signal flow through wires to the handset at the other end. The disc and electromagnet in this second handset turned the message back into sounds. This was how all telephones would work for more than 100 years.

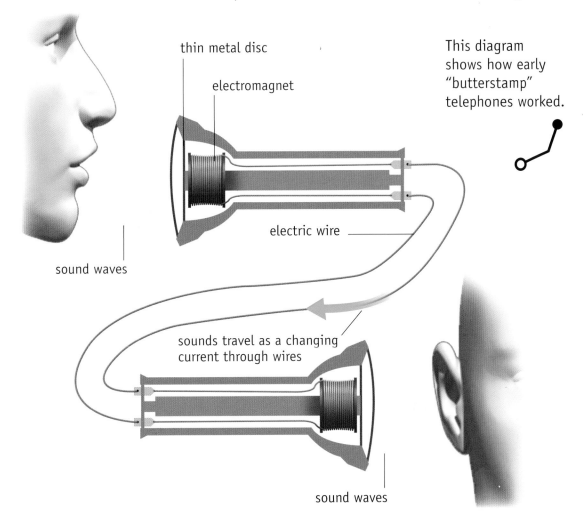

thin metal disc

electromagnet

This diagram shows how early "butterstamp" telephones worked.

sound waves

electric wire

sounds travel as a changing current through wires

sound waves

13

1860–61—The Pony Express carries letters across the United States

1861—Johann Philip Reis makes a telephone, but it does not work properly

1870

1876—Alexander Graham Bell gets the first patent for a successful telephone

1877—The Bell Telephone Company is created

1877—Alexander Graham Bell invents the "butterstamp" telephone

1878—The carbon **microphone** is invented

1870

1880

Alexander Graham Bell *(1847–1922)*

Alexander Graham Bell was born in Scotland. Bell became interested in sound from an early age because his mother was deaf and his father taught deaf people. As a boy, Bell moved his dog's throat to make its growls sound like words!

Bell moved to the United States in 1871 and started to experiment with **telegraphs**. When he invented the telephone, the United States' biggest telegraph company said it was not interested in a "scientific toy"! Bell formed his own telephone company and made the telephone famous by demonstrating it to many people, including Britain's Queen Victoria. By 1915 Bell's first telephone call was so famous that he repeated it to mark the opening of a telephone line that went all the way across the United States. From New York, Bell once again said, "Mr. Watson, come here, I want you," but this time Watson replied that it would take him a week to get there because he was answering from San Francisco, California!

Setbacks

Was Bell truly the inventor of the telephone or just lucky to have gotten the first **patent**? Another U.S. scientist named Elisha Gray tried to get a patent for his telephone just two hours after Bell. Both he and Antonio Meucci said Bell stole their ideas, and both took Bell to court. Gray lost his case and Meucci died before his case was heard.

1888—William Gray creates the first payphone, with coin slots

IMPROVING THE TELEPHONE

Bell's first telephones were huge. The user had to speak into a single handset and then move that handset to his or her ear to listen. However, after Bell's **patent** ran out in 1894, other companies began making different kinds of telephones. By the 1890s, more telephones had two handsets. The user listened through a **receiver** and spoke into a **transmitter**, which sent the sounds along the telephone wires.

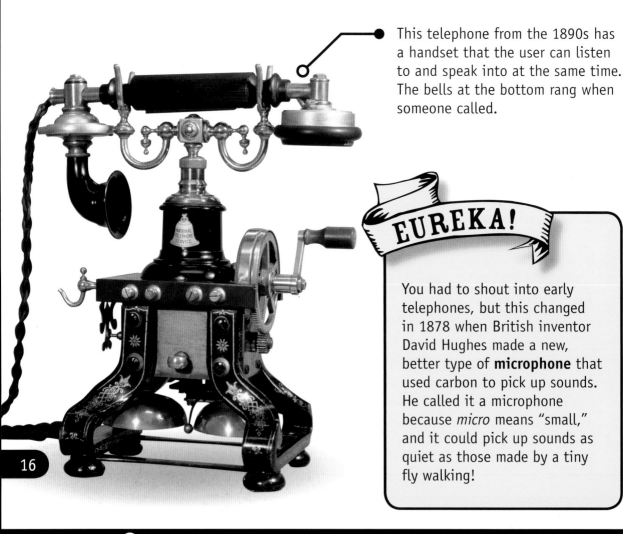

This telephone from the 1890s has a handset that the user can listen to and speak into at the same time. The bells at the bottom rang when someone called.

EUREKA!

You had to shout into early telephones, but this changed in 1878 when British inventor David Hughes made a new, better type of **microphone** that used carbon to pick up sounds. He called it a microphone because *micro* means "small," and it could pick up sounds as quiet as those made by a tiny fly walking!

16

Telephone switchboards

All telephone calls went through a switchboard. When you picked up your phone, a small light told an operator you were waiting. She plugged a wire into your line and asked what number you wanted. She connected you by plugging in wires and taking them out when the conversation was over. This meant that operators could listen in on your calls!

EUREKA!

In 1891 U.S. undertaker Almon Strowger found out that his local telephone operator was passing his calls to a rival undertaker instead. Strowger invented an automatic telephone exchange so callers could use a dial to connect their telephone with another one by themselves.

This photograph shows telephone operators working at a switchboard.

17

Long distance wires

To enable people to speak to each other across long distances, new lines had to be laid. Teams of workers worked hard to lay these lines, even in difficult winter weather. By 1914 there was a continuous line of telephone wires between the west and east coasts of the United States.

The first transatlantic telephone cable was laid in 1956. It traveled under the Atlantic Ocean to connect the United States and the United Kingdom. At first, it could carry only 36 telephone calls at a time. To lay a cable, cable was first unrolled from the back of a ship. Then, because the cable was so heavy, it would sink to the bottom of the sea. Sometimes cables were buried in trenches made by ships dragging an underwater plow.

This photograph shows a cable being dropped from a reel on the back of a ship traveling across the Atlantic Ocean.

EUREKA!

In Great Britain in 1937, the first call was made to the free emergency number 999 for police, medical, or fire departments. In the U.S., the first 911 emergency call was made in 1968.

1914—Telephone lines are laid across the United States

1915—First phone call across the United States is made by Bell and Watson

1910

1920

Changing designs

Since the 1960s, many new kinds of telephones have been made. From 1963 push-button phones made calling numbers quicker because you did not have to wait for a dial to get back into position between numbers. Some push-button phones even glowed in the dark! The first video phones, made in 1964, sent pictures of the people talking. They were very expensive and, even by the 1990s, they were still so slow that it was like talking to a photograph.

Telephones have been designed to have dials or buttons, to be brightly colored, and even to look like hamburgers!

CELL PHONES

The next big development in telephones was the cell phone. These are telephones that work without wires, so people can speak to each other from almost anywhere.

Before cell phones were invented, some people used walkie-talkies. Like cell phones, walkie-talkies work by sending out and receiving messages as **radio waves**. Radio waves are a type of electrical energy that travels through the air in the form of invisible waves. This is the type of energy radio stations use to transmit music to your radio. Walkie-talkies are also known as two-way radios because they have a **transmitter** and a **receiver**. The drawback is that walkie-talkies only work over short distances.

Soldiers used walkie-talkies to **communicate** during World War II.

1937—The first emergency call is made

The first cell phones

U.S. inventor Martin Cooper developed the first successful cell phone in 1973. It was heavy, large, and very expensive. Its **battery** pack gave just 20 minutes of talk time. The Motorola 8000X, made in 1983, was the first one-piece cell phone. It was 30 centimeters (12 inches) long and weighed almost 1 kilogram (2 pounds). It cost $3,500—the same as about $6,500 today.

Early cell phones were bigger than those of today, and people also had to carry battery packs to power them!

Martin Cooper (born 1928)

When U.S. inventor Martin Cooper saw a rival company making carphones by fitting a two-way radio and a power supply into cars, he decided to make a small version you could carry anywhere. He succeeded, and in 1973 made the first ever public call from a handheld cell phone. He called a rival telephone company from a New York street!

How cell phones work

When you talk into a cell phone, it changes **sound waves** from your voice into **radio waves**. The radio waves are sent through the air to a nearby **base station**. This sends the call to a telephone exchange that passes on the call through wires or through radio waves to the person you are calling. When your friend answers, the message travels back through the telephone network to your cell phone, which turns it into speech.

Setbacks

Some doctors think that if people use cell phones too much when they are young, it may cause serious diseases such as brain cancer when they are older. This is because of the radio waves that spread out from the phones and from base stations.

This diagram shows how cell phones work.

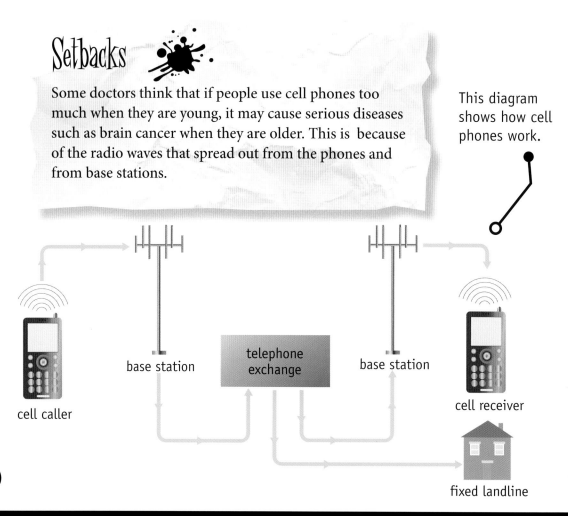

cell caller

base station

telephone exchange

base station

cell receiver

fixed landline

1956—The first telephone cable beneath the Atlantic Ocean is laid, connecting the United States and the United Kingdom

The parts of a cell phone

These are the most important parts of a cell phone:

- SIM card to store information such as phone numbers and to let your network track where you are. SIM stands for "Subscriber Identity Module."

- **circuit** board that contains a **microprocessor** and other parts that act like a tiny computer to control the cell phone

- display screen to show messages and show you what you are typing into the keypad

- keypad buttons that are pressed to send instructions to the microprocessor and circuit board

- **microphone** to turn sound waves into an electrical copy of your voice

- loudspeaker to change electrical signals back into sound waves

- **battery** to provide power to make the phone work

- plastic cover to hold the other parts together.

1962—The first commercial communications **satellite** is launched

1964—The first video phone is invented

1965—The first electronic telephone exchange is developed

1970

Satellites and phones

To send telephone messages around the world, we sometimes use communications **satellites**. These are machines that stay high above Earth. Giant rockets carry satellites into space and then release them. They do not fly off into space because of Earth's **gravity**. Most satellites get their power by using solar cells, parts that turn sunlight into **electricity**.

To use satellites, signals from a cell phone or ordinary phone are sent from a satellite dish to a satellite. The satellite amplifies (strengthens) the signal, then sends it back down to a receiving station on a different part of Earth.

There are hundreds of communications satellites in space that can receive and transmit signals to and from Earth.

1973—The cell phone is invented

This mountian climber is using a GPS phone to figure out where he is.

GPS phones

With a **GPS** (Global Positioning System), no one should ever get lost. A phone with built-in GPS is able to tune in to a number of different satellites that transmit signals to Earth. The GPS phone uses information about where those different satellites are to figure out where it is. GPS cell phones can also help you plan routes and even find your nearest movie theater.

Setbacks

You cannot use cell phones in hospitals or airplanes. **Radio waves** are a type of **electromagnetic** wave. If these waves go through machines in a hospital or computers on an aircraft, they can stop the machines from working properly, which can be very dangerous.

25

1983—The one-piece cell phone is invented

INTO THE FUTURE

Today, some people use their cell phones all the time and hardly ever use an ordinary phone. The latest cell phones are lighter and smaller than ever before. Many of them are more like miniature computers. In addition to using them for talking to people, they can be used to play games, take photographs, watch TV, store and play music and movies, send emails, and to get information from the Internet.

Many cell phones now have touchscreens, so you can switch between functions quickly and easily.

EUREKA!

In 2009 the world's first solar-powered touchscreen phone went on sale. It has a solar panel on the back to make enough **electricity** to power the telephone. You can use your finger to program the phone from the touchscreen.

1991—Digital cell phone networks are in use

1992—The world's first commercial text message is sent

1995—Short Message Service (SMS, or text messaging) is launched

1999—The first cell phones able to send email and connect to the Internet are launched

1990

2000

What's next?

What will telephones be like in the future? Some cell phones may work like a bank card so people can use them to pay for things. They may also be able to check your heartbeat and other health signs and send the information to your doctor if you become sick. Future phones may be able to connect with other machines from a distance. This would mean that if you forgot to set your TV to record your favorite program before leaving home, you could do this from your phone. What would you most like cell phones of the future to be able to do?

This is what some telephone designers think cell phones might look like in the future. They think they might be bendable, see-through, and self-cleaning.

2000—Camera phones go on sale

2007—The iPhone is launched. It is the first cell phone to have a touchscreen.

2009—There are over four billion cell phones in use worldwide

2010

TIMELINE

1746
Jean Nollet proves that electrical signals move fast

1821
Michael Faraday invents the first electric motor

1827
William Sturgeon invents the **electromagnet**

1877
The Bell Telephone Company is created

1876
Alexander Graham Bell gets the first **patent** for a successful telephone

1861
Johann Phillip Reiss makes a telephone, but it does not work properly

1877
Bell invents the "butterstamp" telephone

1878
The carbon **microphone** is invented

1888
William Gray creates the first payphone, with coin slots

1891
Almon Strowger invents the dialing system

1991
Digital cell phone networks are in use

1983
The one-piece cell phone is invented

1973
The cell phone is invented

1965
The first electronic telephone exchange is developed

1992
The world's first commercial text message is sent

1995
The Short Message Service (SMS, or text messaging) is launched

1999
The first cell phones able to send email and connect to the Internet are launched

1831
Faraday shows that **vibrations** on metal objects can be turned into electrical signals

1837
Samuel Morse invents the first successful **telegraph** and the Morse Code

1840
The first postage stamp goes on sale

1860–61
The Pony Express carries letters across the United States

1856
Antonio Meucci makes a telephone system connecting his workshop to his wife's bedroom

1855
An international system for Marine Signal Flags is invented

1914
Telephone lines are laid across the United States

1915
The first phone call across the United States is made by Bell and Watson

1937
The first emergency call is made

1964
The first video phone is invented

1962
The first commercial communications **satellite** is launched

1956
The first telephone cable beneath the Atlantic Ocean is laid, connecting the United States and the United Kingdom

2000
Camera phones go on sale

2007
The iPhone is launched. It is the first cell phone to have a touchscreen.

2009
There are over four billion cell phones in use worldwide

GLOSSARY

acid type of strong liquid chemical

base station antenna on a tower or building that receives and passes on radio wave signals from cell phones

battery device that produces electricity to make a machine work

circuit complete path along which an electric current flows

communicate share or exchange information with someone

current flow of electricity through a wire

electricity form of energy that makes machines work

electromagnet piece of metal that becomes magnetic when electricity passes through it

GPS stands for "Global Positioning System"; system in which signals from a satellite are sent to a device on Earth to tell people exactly where they are in the world

gravity force on Earth that pulls things toward the center of the planet

microphone device that turns sound waves into an electrical copy of your voice so that it can then be amplified, transmitted, or recorded. *Micro* means "small"; *phone* means "voice" or "sound."

microprocessor device that acts as a tiny computer to control a machine

monastery building where monks live. Monks are men who devote their lives to their religion.

patent document issued to someone who invents something new so that other people are not allowed to copy it without permission

radio wave type of energy that travels through the air in the form of invisible waves

receiver device that changes radio waves and other signals into sounds or pictures

satellite electronic device that moves around Earth

sound wave movement of sound energy through the air

steamship ship powered by a coal-burning steam engine

telegraph system of sending messages as electrical signals along wires

transmitter device for sending electrical signals such as radio and TV signals

vibrate move up and down or back and forth very quickly

FIND OUT MORE

Books

Fandel, Jennifer. *Inventions and Discovery: Alexander Graham Bell and the Telephone*. North Mankato, Minn.: Capstone, 2007.

Kummer, Patricia K. *Inventions that Shaped the World: The Telephone*. New York: Franklin Watts, 2006.

Micklos, John. *Time for Kids Biographies: Alexander Graham Bell: Inventor of the Telephone*. New York: HarperCollins, 2006.

Websites

Discover more about Bell, Gray, and other inventors at:
www.pbs.org/wgbh/amex/telephone/index.html

Find out more telephone history and read biographies of important inventors at:
http://inventors.about.com/od/bstartinventors/a/telephone.htm

Places to visit

The Museum of Communications
7000 East Marginal Way South
Seattle, Washington 98108
www.museumofcommunications.org

Museum of Science
Science Park
Boston, Massachusetts 02114
www.mos.org

INDEX